S0-AEE-924

Explore and Draw

BIG CATS

DRAWING AND READING

Monica Halpern

Rourke
Educational Media

rourkeeducationalmedia.com

© 2011 Rourke Educational Media
All rights reserved. No part of this book may be
reproduced or utilized in any form or by any means,
electronic or mechanical
including photocopying, recording, or by any
information storage and retrieval system without
permission in writing from the publisher.
www.rourkeeducationalmedia.com

Editor: Penny Dowdy
Art Direction: Cheena Yadav (Q2AMedia)
Designer: Suzena Samuel, Jasmeen Kaur
(Q2AMedia)
Illustrator: Vinay Kumar Sharma
Picture researcher: Rajeev Parmar (Q2AMedia)

Picture credits:
t=top b=bottom c=centre l=left r=right
Cover: Malou Leontsinis/Shutterstock
Back Cover: Rod Kaye/Istockphoto, Roessler Carl/
Photolibrary, Cretolamna/Shutterstock, Nathan
Jones/Istockphoto, David Lewis/Istockphoto,
Tischenko Irina/Shutterstock, Malou Leontsinis/
Shutterstock, Radoslav Stoilov/Shutterstock, Close
Encounters Photography/Shutterstock, CTR Photos/
Shutterstock.
Title page: Nina Malyna/Shutterstock, Awe
Inspiring Images/Shutterstock, Vladimir Wrangel/
Shutterstock, Vladimir Sazonov/Shutterstock,
Timothy Craig Lubcke/Shutterstock, Tania
A/Shutterstock, Ipatov/Shutterstock, EML/
Shutterstock, Nickolay Stanev/Shutterstock, Peter
Wey/Shutterstock, Four Oaks/Shutterstock, Sasha
Podgorny/Shutterstock, Ekaterina Starshaya/
Shutterstock, Oleg Kozlov/Shutterstock.
Insides: Nina Malyna/Shutterstock, Awe
Inspiring Images/Shutterstock, Vladimir Wrangel/
Shutterstock, Vladimir Sazonov/Shutterstock,
Timothy Craig Lubcke/Shutterstock, Tania
A/Shutterstock, Ipatov/Shutterstock, EML/
Shutterstock, Nickolay Stanev/Shutterstock, Peter
Wey/Shutterstock, Four Oaks/Shutterstock, Sasha
Podgorny/Shutterstock, Ekaterina Starshaya/
Shutterstock, Oleg Kozlov/Shutterstock.
Nina Malyna/Shutterstock, Awe Inspiring Images/
Shutterstock, Vladimir Wrangel/Shutterstock,
Vladimir Sazonov/Shutterstock, Timothy Craig
Lubcke/Shutterstock, Tania A/Shutterstock, Ipatov/
Shutterstock, EML/Shutterstock, Nickolay Stanev/
Shutterstock, Peter Wey/Shutterstock, Four Oaks/
Shutterstock, Sasha Podgorny/Shutterstock,
Ekaterina Starshaya/Shutterstock, Oleg Kozlov/
Shutterstock: 4- 24, Tom Brakefield/Photolibrary:
6, Bluedeep/ Dreamstime: 7, Bill Bachmann/
Photolibrary: 10, Juan Carlos Munoz/Photolibrary:
11, Andrea Poole/Dreamstime: 14, Neelsky/
Shutterstock: 15, Alan & Sandy Carey/Photolibrary:
18, Gerald Hinde/ABPL /Photolibrary: 19.

Q2AMedia Art Bank: Cover, Title Page, 4-5, 8-9,
12-13, 16-17, 20-21, Back Cover

**Library of Congress Cataloging-in-Publication
Data**

Becker, Ann, 1965 Oct. 6-
Big Cats: explore and draw / Monica Halpern.
p. cm. – (Explore and draw)
Includes index.
ISBN 978-1-61590-255-2 (hard cover)
ISBN 978-1-61590-495-2 (soft cover)
1. Big Cats in art–Juvenile literature. 2. Drawing–
Technique–Juvenile literature.
I. Title. II. Title: Explore and draw.
NC825.A4B43 2009
743'.8962913334–dc22
2009021617

Rourke Educational Media
Printed in the United States of America,
North Mankato, Minnesota

Contents

Technique

Before you start drawing big cats, let's talk about how to use shapes.

1

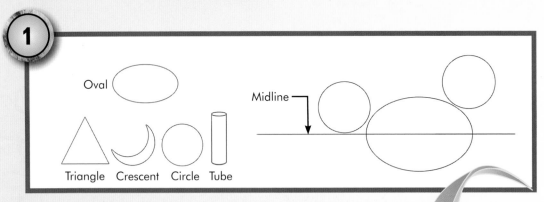

Oval

Midline

Triangle Crescent Circle Tube

Ovals, triangles, crescents, circles, and tubes are the basic shapes used to draw big cats. Draw a midline to form the center of your cat. Add a large oval around it for the body. Add two circles to show the cat's head and hips.

2

Now, draw tubes with small circles at the ends for the legs and paws. Then, lightly draw guidelines to connect the shapes. You have now drawn the **framework** of the big cat.

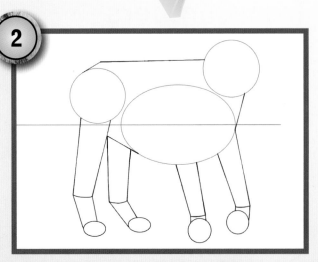

3

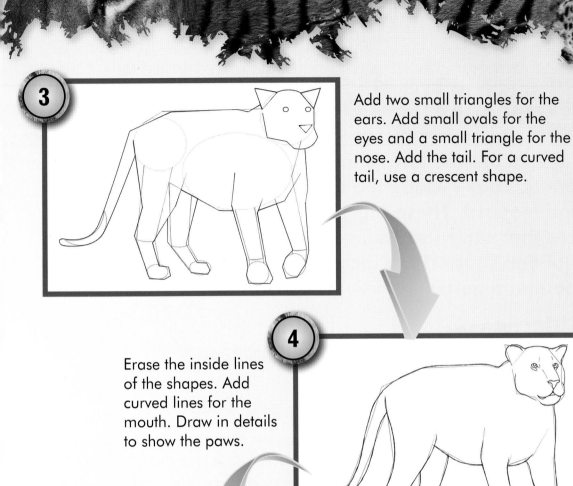

Add two small triangles for the ears. Add small ovals for the eyes and a small triangle for the nose. Add the tail. For a curved tail, use a crescent shape.

4

Erase the inside lines of the shapes. Add curved lines for the mouth. Draw in details to show the paws.

5

Shade your drawing using light and dark tones to show the fur and give dimension. Add details, such as the whiskers.

Meet the Big Cats

Big cats are the largest members of the cat family. They include the tiger, lion, jaguar, and leopard. These big cats are the only cats that can roar. There are other big cats that don't roar. They include the cheetah, mountain lion, and snow leopard.

Big cats need to be fast runners to catch their **prey**.

Big Cats Run

The cheetah is the world's fastest **mammal**. It can run at speeds of up to 70 miles per hour (113 kilometers per hour). The cheetah can go from 0 to 60 mph (96 kph) in only three seconds. Its **acceleration** is faster than any car.

Leopards like to hunt from trees. Their spotted coats blend in with the leaves.

Big Cats Roar

Roaring cats have a special **larynx** or voice box. The larynx is an organ in the neck of roaring cats. This is where sound is produced.

Big Cats Hide

Big cats use **camouflage** to help them hunt. The color and markings on their fur help them blend in with the grass and trees. Their **prey** doesn't see them until it is too late.

Big Cats Are Strong

Big cats are strong in different ways. The mountain lion has **muscular** hind legs that are longer than its front legs. It uses those strong hind legs to leap across the rocky mountains. The mountain lion can leap straight up 18 feet (5.4 meters) from a standing position. It will leap onto the back of its prey and kill it with a bite to the neck.

Draw a Cheetah

The fast cheetah has a beautiful spotted coat, a lean body, and a long, curved tail.

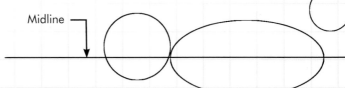

Midline

1 Draw a midline. Add an oval for the chest and midsection of the body. Add circles at each end of the oval for the hips and head.

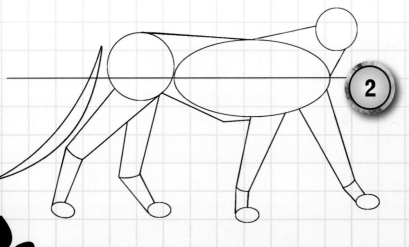

2 Draw tubes with small circles at the ends for the legs and paws. Draw a crescent for the tail. Connect the body to the tail and head with light guidelines.

3 Draw small triangles for the ears and nose. Add small ovals for the eyes.

4 Erase the shape lines. Smooth the guidelines. Add detail to show the **muzzle** and paws.

5 Draw a lot of small dots along the cheetah's back, sides, and legs to show the cheetah's coat. Add shading to give the cheetah dimension.

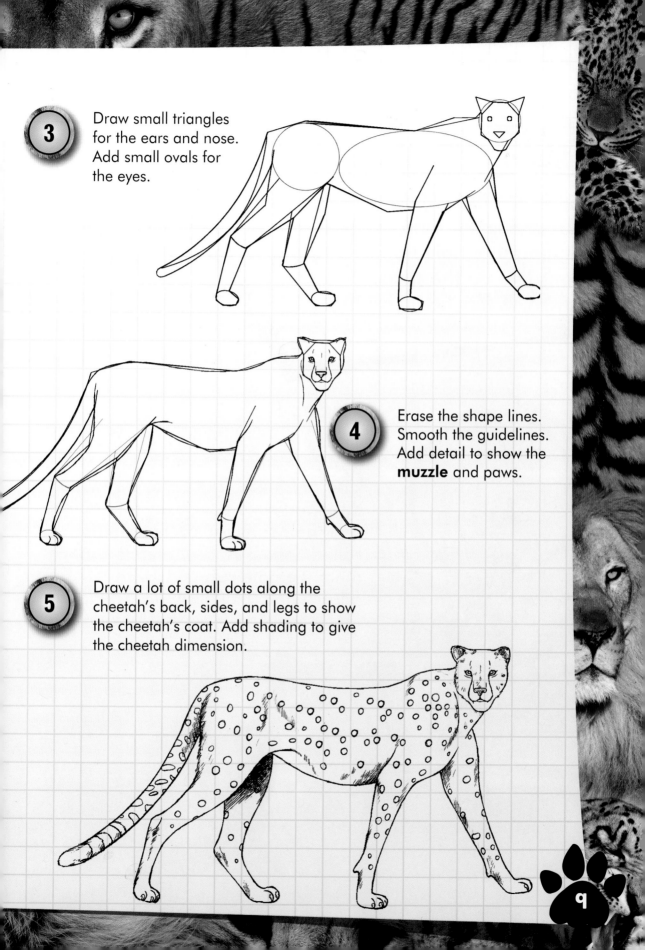

King of the Cats

Lions are the only cats with manes. A mane is the long fringe of hair circling the male lion's head. Most lions live on the **grasslands** of Africa. A few lions live in Asia.

Prides

Lions are the only cats that live in groups, called **prides**. Prides are a kind of family. There may be two or three males, a dozen or so females, and their cubs. All of the females, called lionesses, are related to each other. Female cubs stay with the pride when they grow up. Young males leave to form their own pride.

A pride's territory covers about 100 square miles (259 square kilometers).

Male Lions

Only male lions have manes. This makes them look big and strong. One of their jobs is to protect the pride's territory. They do this by roaring to warn other animals away. The males will also chase off any animals that want to harm them.

Hunting for Food

Female lions do most of the hunting. They usually hunt at night. Unlike other big cats, lions hunt in groups. Their prey includes antelopes, zebras, and other large animals. Since some of their prey are fast, lions use teamwork to catch them. But teamwork ends once food is on the table. The pride argues over the best tidbits, with the cubs getting the leftovers.

The lion's larynx is the longest of the big cats. That is why the lion has the loudest roar.

Draw a Lion

The male lion has a big head that looks even bigger because of his mane. His mane makes the lion special.

1 Draw a vertical and a horizontal midline. Add a small circle for the head and a larger circle for the mane.

2 Draw a triangle for the nose. Draw circles for the ears and smaller circles for the eyes. Draw a six-sided shape inside the bigger circle to form the lion's mane.

 Add detail to the
nose, muzzle, and
eyes. Add a lot of
curving lines to show
the lion's furry mane.

3 Draw a half-square
shape for the muzzle.
Add angles to the lion's
face. Draw rough lines
to begin the mane.

5 Add whiskers. Then,
shade your lion to
make it look natural
and to add dimension.

Tigers, the Biggest Cats

Tigers are the world's biggest cats. They can reach almost 11 feet in length (3.3 meters). They are also the heaviest big cats. They use their powerful legs and shoulders to pull down large prey.

Tigers Have Stripes

Tigers have long, thick, reddish coats with white bellies. They are easy to recognize because of their stripes. Their stripes can be brown, gray, or black. Most tigers have over 100 stripes. No two tigers have the same pattern of stripes.

The largest cats are Siberian tigers. They can weigh up to 660 pounds (300 kilograms).

Tigers' Habitats

Tigers live in many different **habitats**, from open grasslands to swamps. Their habitat always has three features. It has good **cover**, a place for the tiger to hide while hunting. It is close to water. There is plenty of prey.

Tigers Hunt

Tigers are meat-eaters. Their main prey are deer and wild pig. Unlike lions, tigers live and hunt alone. They are most active at night. They use camouflage to help them hunt. When prey comes along, tigers leap out and grab it. Male tigers will let nearby females and cubs eat first.

Tigers hunt by sight and hearing, not by smell.

Draw a Tiger

Imagine meeting a tiger in the forest! No one can mistake that noble head for any other creature.

1 Draw a vertical and a horizontal midline. Add a larger circle for the head and a smaller circle for the mouth.

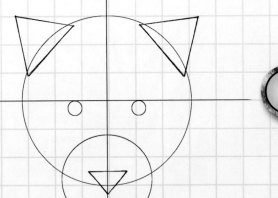

2 Draw two small circles for eyes. Add a small triangle to form the nose. Next, draw triangles for the ears.

3 Add two lines below the nose to form the muzzle. Soften the shape lines to make the head and ears look more natural. Add two lines on each side of the head to suggest the body. Draw a crescent, a half circle, at both sides of the head to form the thick fur around the jaw.

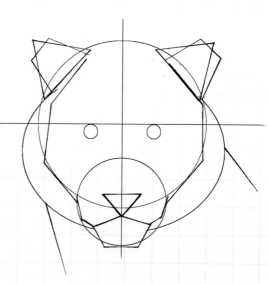

4 Erase the unneeded shape lines. Add detail to the eyes, nose, and mouth.

5 Add whiskers. Draw thin, dark crescent shapes around the tiger's head to show its stripes. Make your tiger look real by shading it to show fur.

Tree Climbers

Leopards are the smallest of the four big cats. They are the strongest tree-climber of the big cats. They can carry large prey up a tree. They do that to keep other **predators** from getting a free lunch!

The Spotted Leopard

Leopards have short legs and a long, muscular body. They can jump more than 20 feet (6 meters) forward or 10 feet (3 meters) straight up! Most leopards are light colored with dark spots. These spots are called rosettes because they are shaped like a rose. The leopards' spots help them blend in with their surroundings. They can hide from their prey.

Black leopards also have dark spots, but the spots are hard to see.

Leopards often hide in a tree and wait for prey to come along.

The Leopard's Habitats

Leopards live in many parts of Africa and Asia. Like tigers, they live alone. Leopards are very **adaptable**. They can live in many habitats, from rainforests to deserts. Their favorite habitat is dense bush in rocky areas or forests. Leopards like water and are fine swimmers.

Leopards Hunt

Leopards will eat just about anything, as long as it's meat. They don't try to compete for food with tigers and lions. Instead, they often hunt at different times of the day and in different areas. They usually rest during the day and hunt at night.

Draw a Leopard

The leopard has a wonderful spotted coat.

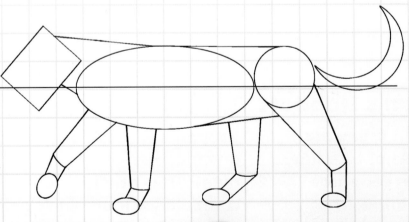

1 Draw a midline and an oval for the body. Add a circle for the hips and a square for the head.

2 Draw a crescent for the tail. Draw tubes with small circles at the ends for the legs and paws. Add light guidelines to connect the body to the tail and head.

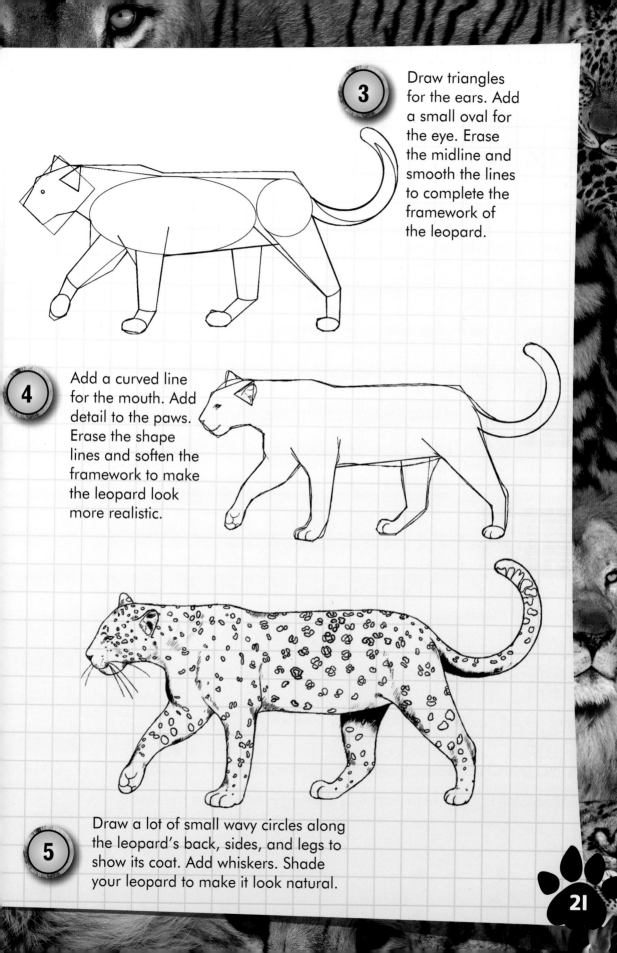

3 Draw triangles for the ears. Add a small oval for the eye. Erase the midline and smooth the lines to complete the framework of the leopard.

4 Add a curved line for the mouth. Add detail to the paws. Erase the shape lines and soften the framework to make the leopard look more realistic.

5 Draw a lot of small wavy circles along the leopard's back, sides, and legs to show its coat. Add whiskers. Shade your leopard to make it look natural.

Glossary

acceleration (ak-sel-uh-RAY-shun): an increase in speed

adaptable (uh-DAP-tuh-bul): able to change in new situations

camouflage (KAM-uh-flahzh): coloring that makes animals, people, or objects look like their surroundings

cover (KUV-ur): something that hides or protects

framework (FRAYM-wurk): a structure that gives shape or support to something

grasslands (GRAS-landz): lands covered mainly with grass

habitats (HAB-uh-tatz): places where animals or plants naturally live and grow

larynx (LAR-inks): the top part of the windpipe; holds the vocal cords

mammal (MAM-uhl): a kind of animal that is warm-blooded and has a backbone

muscular (MUS-kyuh-lur): having strong or well-developed muscles

muzzle (MUZ-uhl): the nose, mouth, and jaws of an animal

predators (PRED-uh-turz): animals that kill other animals for food

prey (PRAY): an animal that is hunted by another animal for food

prides (PRIGHDZ): lion families that live together

shade (SHAYD): to make part of a drawing darker than the rest

Index

Websites to Visit

www.bigcats.com
This site provides facts, photos, and recent news about big cats.

www.awf.org
The African Wildlife Foundation tells about the physical characteristics, habitat, and behavior of big cats.

www.sandiegozoo.org
The San Diego Zoo gives lots of interesting facts, photos, sounds, maps, and fun information about big cats.

About the Author
Monica Halpern has worked in publishing for over 20 years. She has written several books for kids. She especially likes to write about animals. Big cats are among her favorite animals. She lives outside Boston with her husband and her dog.

About the Illustrator
Vinay Kumar Sharma has illustrated a number of children's books. He has a Masters in Fine Arts. Vinay draws primarily realistic art. He loves drawing the world around him. Vinay lives with his family in New Delhi. He has been working for Q2A Media for three years.